Finding Things from A to Z

Written and Illustrated by Beverly Wulforst

4/18/14

Lauri - Our time together at SCAD
is one that I will always treasure!
Your friendship, support and
encouragement - both personally and
professionally - are gifts that
helped me - and continue to help me &
many others, I'm sure, on this
amazing and creative journey that
is life! Miss you!

Love,
Beverly

This book is dedicated to my first grade teacher, Mrs. Freeman, who encouraged me to follow my love of reading and gave me the opportunity to do so.

There are 26 letters in this rhyme

With clues in-between to help you find

Many things starting from A to Z

In this little letter menagerie

Find 11 things

that start with A

One of them helps

keep the doctor away

Acorn, airplane, alligator, amoré, anchor, angel, ant, apple, asparagus, astronaut, aviator

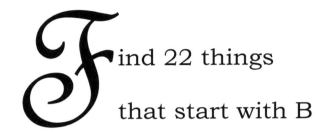

ind 22 things

that start with B

One of them has "eyes"

but cannot see!

Balloon, bananas, barn, baseball, basket, bathtub, beaver, bee, beetle, bell, bicycle, birdhouse, black-eyed peas, blueberries, bluebird, book, bowl, bubbles, bucket, bull, butterfly, buttons

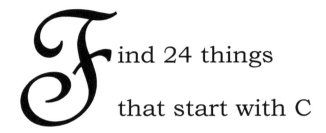

ind 24 things

that start with C

You should eat some of these

to stay healthy

Cabbages, camel, carrots, castle, cat, caterpillar, chair, chameleon, cheese, cherry, chickens, chipmunk, chocolate candy, chocolate chips, clouds, cookies, corn, cow, creamer, crescent moon, cricket, crown, cupcake, curtains

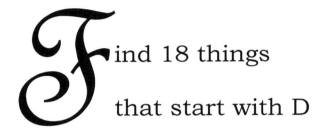

Find 18 things

that start with D

One of them is

sweet and sugary

Daffodils, daisies, daybreak, deck, deer, dock, dog, doll, dolphin, donkey, door, doughnut, dove, dragon, dragonfly, dress, drum, duck

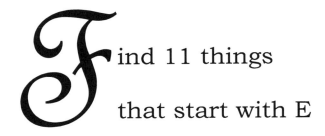

Find 11 things

that start with E

They all live as one

in harmony

Eagle, ears, earth, egg, egret, elephant, elk, emperor, envelope, Eskimo, eyes

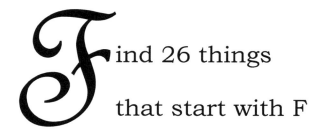ind 26 things

that start with F

One brings good luck

that you can pick for yourself

Face, feathers, fairy, farmer, fawn, fence, fern, ferris wheel, fingers, fins, fireworks, fish, fishing pole, flag, flag pole, flamingo, flip-flops, flowers, flute, fly, football, fountain, four-leaf clover, four-legged stool, fox, frog

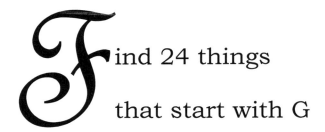

Find 24 things

that start with G

You can see two running,

filled with glee

Galoshes, gate, gazebo, geraniums, gingerbread man, gingerbread trim, girl, glasses, goat, golden retriever, goldfish, goldfish bowl, goose, gopher, grandma, grapefruit, grape vine, grapes, grass, grasshopper, grin, ground, grove, guinea pig

*F*ind 42 things

that start with H

Some of them

you might like to chase

Hair, hair bow, halo, hammer, hammock, hamster, hands,
handstand, harmonica, harp, hat, hawk, hayloft, hayride, heart,
heaven, heavenly gates, hedge, hedgehog, heifer, hen, henhouse,
herbs, hills, hive, hoe, hog, holly, hollyhocks, honey, honey bees,
honey jar, hopscotch, hornets, hornets' nest, horns, horse, hose,
house, hula hoop, hyacinth, hydrangeas

$\mathcal{F}$ind 15 things

that start with I

One likes to climb,

one likes to fly

Ibex, ibis, ice cream, iceberg, igloo, iguana, inchworm, ink, ink bottle, insects, iris, iron, ironing board, island, ivy

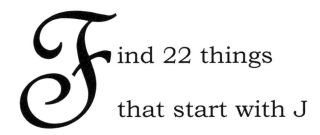

Find 22 things

that start with J

Several of them

like to laugh and play

Jack Russell terrier, jackal, jacket, jack-in-the-box, jack-o-lantern, jaguar, jar, jasmine, jacks, jeans, jelly beans, jellyfish, jester, jet, jewels, jockey, jug, juggling balls, jump rope, jungle, juniper, Jupiter

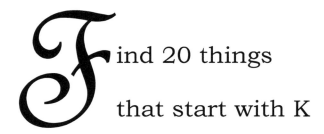

*F*ind 20 things

that start with K

You can see one flying

far, far away

Kale, kangaroo, kart, kettle, key, keys (piano), keystone, kid, kilt, kindling, king, kiss, kite, kitten, kiwi, knight, knitting needles, knot, koala bear, kumquat

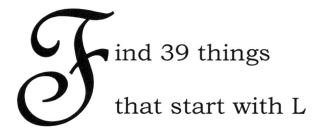

Find 39 things

that start with L

One of them has

a black and white tail

Lace, ladder, ladle, ladybugs, lake, lamb, lantern, lark, laundry, lead, leaf, legs, lemons, lemur, letter, lettuce, library, licorice, lid, light bulb, lighthouse, lightning, lightning bugs, lilacs, lilies, lima beans, limes, line, links, lion, lips, list, lizard, llama, lobster, lock, logs, log cabin, lollipops

Find 16 things

that start with M

One loves to swing,

two love to swim

Mail, mailbox, manatee, map, mermaid, mirror, mole, monkey, moon, moose, morning glory, moth, mountains, mouse, mouth, mushroom

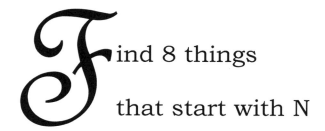

ind 8 things

that start with N

One is being held

by the bride named Jen

Necklace, neighborhood, newlyweds, newspaper, Niagara Falls,
night, nose, nosegay

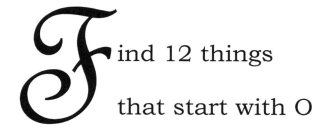

Find 12 things

that start with O

One says "hoot"

and is in the know

Ocean, octagon, octopus, olives, oranges, orangutan, orchid, ornaments, ostrich, otter, owl, oyster

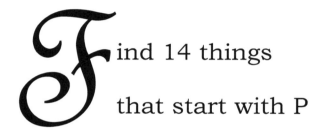

ind 14 things

that start with P

One spreads his feathers

for all to see

Palm tree, pancakes, peach, peacock, pear, pelican, penguin, pig, pineapple, plum, pomegranate, pond, porcupine, pyramids

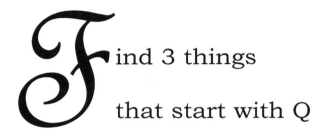

Find 3 things

that start with Q

One wears a crown

that is quite new

Quail, queen, quilt

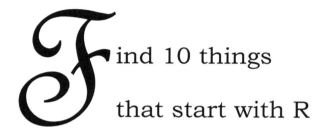

Find 10 things

that start with R

One likes to crow

and be the star

Rabbit, raccoon, radish, rain, rhinoceros, road, rocket,
roller coaster, rooster, ruler

Find 34 things

that start with S

One likes to slither

more than the rest

Saddle, saddle oxford, sailboat, sand, sand dollar, school bus, schoolhouse, scooter, sea, sea serpent, seashell, seesaw, sheep, shoestring, sidewalk, skunk, sled, slide, snail, snake, snow, snowman, sock, soil, space, space ship, spider, star, street, sun, sunflowers, sunset, swimmer, swings

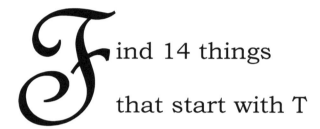

$\mathcal{F}$ind 14 things

that start with T

One you can swing on

from a tree

Teapot, tie, tiger, tire swing, tomatoes, tooth, traffic light, train, T-rex, triangles, trumpet, tulip, turkey, turtle

Find 5 things

that start with U

Several live

in the ocean blue

Ukulele, umbrella, unicorn, Uranus, urchins

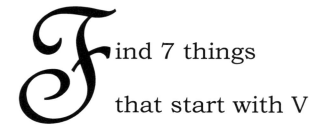

Find 7 things

that start with V

One must be played

in just the right key

Vase, vault, vine, violets, violin, volcano, vulture

*F*ind 22 things

that start with W

One you can open

for a better view

Wagon, wallpaper, walnut, walrus, wand, wasp, water, water wheel, waterfall, weeping willow tree, whale, wheat, wheels, windmill, window, wings, wink, witch, wizard, wolf, woodpecker, worm

Find 2 things

that start with X

One you can see through

as you would expect

X-ray, xylophone

Find 7 things

that start with Y

One of them likes

to wave goodbye

Yacht, yak, yardstick, yarn, yodeler, yolk, yoyo

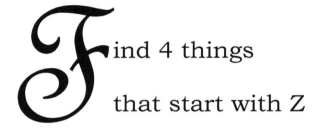

Find 4 things

that start with Z

One likes to snooze

under a tree

Zebra, zigzag, zipper, zucchini

$\mathcal{N}$ow that's just

the beginning

As you can see

Of this little letter menagerie

Think of all the things

from A to Z

And then look them up

In the dictionary!

Special thanks to my devoted husband, Steve, my two wonderful sons, Nick and Alex, and my amazing mother, Sylvia, for all of your support and encouragement during the creation of this book.

Made in the USA
Charleston, SC
26 August 2013